PRAYING MANTIS

ROSEATE SPOONBILL

SMALL-SPOTTED
GENET

THE BIG BOOK OF
ANIMALS

Sheila Hanly

DK

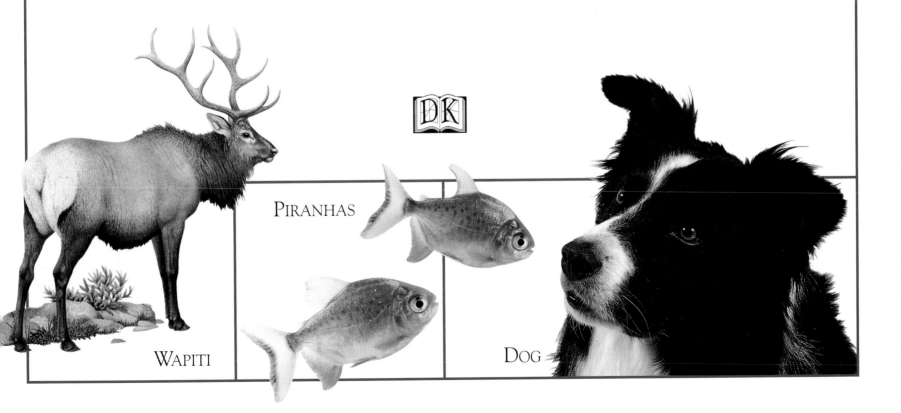

PIRANHAS

WAPITI

DOG

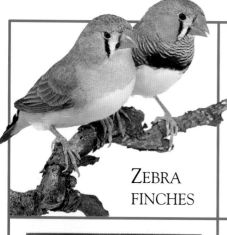

ZEBRA FINCHES

MONK SEAL

JAPANESE MACAQUE

COYOTE

RED KANGAROO

DK

A DK PUBLISHING BOOK

www.dk.com

The Big Book of Animals was designed by **Roger Priddy** and **Helen Melville**, with extra help from **Mary Sandberg. Rachel Wardley** edited the text, assisted by **Jenny Síklos. Joanne Beardwell** and **Felicity Crowe** did the picture research helped by **Joanne Houghton**, while **Josie Alabaster** handled the production process. **Theresa Greenaway**, an animal expert, checked the book for accuracy. **Kristin Ward** edited the US version. The illustrations were painted by **Kenneth Lilly**.

Photography for DK was done by the following people: Peter Anderson, Paul Bricknell, Geoff Brightling, Jane Burton, Gordon Clayton, Andy Crawford, Geoff Dann, Phillip Dowell, Mike Dunning, Neil Fletcher, Frank Greenaway, Marc Henrie, Colin Keates, Dave King, Cyril Laubscher, Gary Lewis, JF Reynolds, Karl Shone, Steve Shott, Kim Taylor, and Jerry Young

First American Edition, 1997
4 6 8 10 9 7 5 3
DK Publishing, Inc.
95 Madison Avenue
New York, New York 10016

A catalog record is available from the Library of Congress.

ISBN 0-7894-1485-6

Color reproduction by Colourscan, Singapore.
Printed in Spain by
Artes Gráficas Toledo, S.A.U.
D.L. TO: 43-2000

CONTENTS

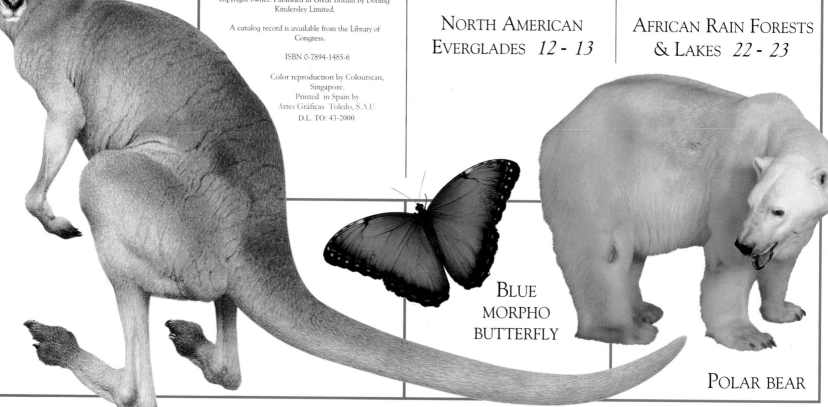

BLUE MORPHO BUTTERFLY

POLAR BEAR

TOUCAN

ELECTRIC RAY

MOON MOTH

LANNER FALCON

SALLYLIGHTFOOT CRAB

HOWLER MONKEY

RINGTAIL OPOSSUM

Where in the World?

The animals that you will see in this book live all over the world in different environments or habitats. There are ten main types of habitats.

GRASSLANDS
The hot African savanna, the cooler North American prairies, the pampas in South America, and the Asian steppe are all types of grasslands, or flat, grassy plains.

SCRUBLANDS
Hot, dusty scrublands are found in southern Europe, Australia, and California.

CONIFEROUS FORESTS
The largest coniferous forests stretch right across the top of North America, Europe, and Asia. Conifer trees have needlelike leaves that stay on the tree all year round.

ICY LANDS
The Arctic and Antarctic are icy, windy places where it is very difficult for animals to survive.

RAIN FORESTS
More than half of all the different animals and plants in the world live in these hot, moist jungles.

DECIDUOUS FORESTS
Deciduous forests grow in temperate parts of the northern hemisphere. Deciduous trees lose their leaves in winter.

DESERTS
In deserts it hardly ever rains, so whether it is hot or cold, the animals that live in them have to be able to survive with practically no water at all.

MOUNTAINS
Mountains are in both hot and cold parts of the world, but all mountains are very cold near their peaks.

MARSHES AND SWAMPS
Wet, soggy places near lakes and rivers are called marshes or swamps. The Everglades in North America is one of the largest areas of marshland in the world.

THE OCEAN
From deep oceans to shallow coral reefs, salty seawater teems with underwater animals.

Animal Groups

There are more than a million different, named animals in the world, but scientists think that there could be four times as many that have not yet been discovered. Animals have certain things in common – they breathe, feed, grow, and have babies – but they also have many differences. To help people talk about and study animals, they have been divided into six groups.

MAMMALS
All young mammals, from whales and dogs to kangaroos and humans, feed on their mothers' milk. They breathe air, and their bodies are covered with fur or hair.

BIRDS
Birds are the only animals with feathers. They lay eggs, with hard, protective shells, which they keep warm until the chicks hatch out. Birds have wings, and most can fly.

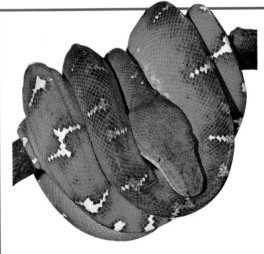

REPTILES
Most reptiles live on land. They breathe air, and their bodies are covered in dry, scaly skin. Crocodiles, snakes, lizards, and turtles are all reptiles.

FISH
Equipped with gills that take in oxygen, fish are able to live and breathe in water. They have fins to help them swim, and bodies covered in skin or overlapping scales.

AMPHIBIANS
Most adult amphibians live on land, but breed in water. They usually have soft, moist skin. They start life as eggs, then turn into tadpoles before reaching adulthood.

INVERTEBRATES
Invertebrates are a huge group of animals that do not have backbones. They come in all shapes and sizes, from tiny insects, snails, and crabs, to giant squid.

The Arctic

ARCTIC FOX
The Arctic fox's brown fur turns white in winter. This helps it hide in the snow, protecting it from enemies.

NORWAY LEMMING
Very common in the Arctic, these lemmings live in burrows.

POLAR BEAR
A polar bear lives and hunts alone. It waits at holes in ice for a seal to pop its head out to breathe, then kills it with a blow from its huge paw.

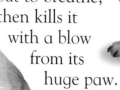

ARCTIC TERN
After raising its chicks in the Arctic summer, this tern flies all the way to the Antarctic, on the other side of the world, to enjoy summer again!

MUSK OXEN
Musk oxen form a circle around their babies when they are threatened. Then they face outward to defend themselves with their long, sharp horns.

GREENLAND CARIBOU
A caribou's broad hooves and waterproof coat are perfect for life in thick snow. Caribou live in large herds, traveling south as it gets colder.

SNOWY OWL
The snowy owl will feed on any small animal it comes across, but its main food is lemmings.

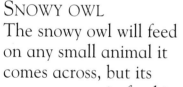

WALRUS
Walruses spend most of their time sunbathing on ice. Layers of fat keep them warm.

PUFFIN
A puffin's bill can hold up to 12 fish at a time. It is also brightly colored in the breeding season to help the puffin attract a mate.

HOODED SEAL
This seal spends most of its life in the sea, hunting for fish and squid to eat.

North American Rockies

BOBCAT
A bobcat's spotted coat helps it blend into its surroundings so it can creep up on prey. It usually eats rabbits and hares, but is strong enough to kill a deer, which makes a huge meal.

SNOWSHOE HARE
This hare has very furry feet, like snowshoes with fur, to stop it from sinking into snow.

GRIZZLY BEAR
Huge and powerful, the grizzly bear can kill an animal as big as a moose with its sharp front claws. It stands upright for a better view of its prey.

BIGHORN SHEEP
A bighorn sheep has a shaggy coat to keep it warm in the mountains.

WAPITI
The wapiti is a deer with huge antlers that can weigh more than 22 lb (10 kg). It has a white patch on its rear end.

PTARMIGAN
In winter, these birds grow white feathers to match their snowy habitat. In summer, the female grows brown feathers to hide her when she sits on her nest.

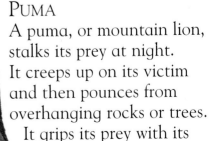

PUMA
A puma, or mountain lion, stalks its prey at night. It creeps up on its victim and then pounces from overhanging rocks or trees. It grips its prey with its long claws and kills it with a bite to the throat.

GRAY WOLF
Wolves hunt in packs, stalking a single animal for long distances.

North American Forests, Lakes, and Prairies

NORTH AMERICAN BADGER
A solitary animal, the badger snarls and growls when it is frightened.

WOLVERINE
Strong and fierce, the wolverine has a powerful bite. It can run for over 40 mi (64 km) nonstop when chasing prey.

BURROWING OWL
This tiny owl lives in an underground burrow that it digs with its feet.

WHOOPING CRANE
This crane gets its name from its loud, buglelike call. It is very rare, nesting only in a remote area of Canada.

OPOSSUM
To fool an enemy, the opossum pretends that it is dead. This act is called "playing possum," and the opossum can keep it up for hours on end.

MOOSE
The biggest deer of all, a moose's broad hooves and long legs help it wade through snow or mud in search of food.

PRAIRIE DOG
Prairie dogs are a type of rodent. They live in groups in huge networks of underground tunnels.

SAGE GROUSE
In spring, the male sage grouse puffs out his chest, shakes his tail, and booms loudly – all to attract a female.

CHIPMUNKS
The chipmunk carries food to its burrow in large pouches in its cheeks. In winter, when food is scarce, it survives by falling into an extra-deep sleep, called hibernation.

North American Forests, Lakes, and Prairies

RACCOON
The raccoon eats all sorts of foods, from fruit, berries, and nuts to eggs, crabs, and insects. It spends much of its time trying to catch underwater creatures with its hands.

BEAVER
The beaver gnaws through tree trunks with its sharp teeth. It uses the wood to build dams across rivers and a lodge for its family.

BALD EAGLES
Male and female bald eagles perform an amazing courtship display. They lock talons and perform somersaults in midair.

MONARCH BUTTERFLY
In fall, these butterflies fly 2,000 mi (3,219 km) to spend winter in the Mexican sun.

BLUE JAY
The blue jay has a useful habit. It buries nuts in the ground to eat later. Sometimes these nuts sprout and grow into trees. This helps forests spread.

BISON
Thousands of bison once roamed the American prairies, but now few herds are left. In winter, some herds move south, looking for grass, while others stay where they are, digging into the snow to uncover food.

COYOTE
Coyotes live in groups. They use sound, smell, and sight to communicate with each other.

North American Deserts

WESTERN DIAMOND-BACK RATTLESNAKE
This snake rattles the rings of hard skin on its tail to scare away big animals that might step on it.

KANGAROO RAT
The kangaroo rat never drinks. It gets all the liquid it needs from its food.

SWALLOWTAIL BUTTERFLY
This butterfly has long tails on its back wings that look like a swallow's tail.

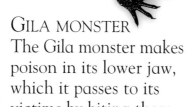

GILA MONSTER
The Gila monster makes poison in its lower jaw, which it passes to its victims by biting them.

COLLARED LIZARD
The brightly colored collared lizard shelters in rock crevices at night, but comes out in the morning to sunbathe.

GILA WOODPECKER
The Gila woodpecker pecks a hole in a cactus stem for a nest. In addition to being cool, the nest is protected by the cactus thorns.

SIDEWINDER SNAKE
The sidewinder gets its name from the way it slithers sideways over the sand. To keep cool during the day, it lies beneath the surface of the sand. Sidewinders are poisonous and can be aggressive if disturbed.

COLLARED PECCARY
Despite their looks, peccaries are not wild pigs. They have stumpy tails and live in groups of 25-30 other peccaries.

SPOTTED SKUNK
If attacked, the skunk stands on its forefeet and sprays a smelly liquid into its enemy's eyes.

North American Deserts

DESERT TORTOISE
It's very difficult for an attacker to reach a tortoise's body once its legs and head are tucked up inside its shell.

BLACK-TAILED JACK RABBIT
The huge surface area of a jack rabbit's ears help give off body heat so the rabbit stays cool. Jack rabbits eat plant foods such as bark, buds, and grass. They will even eat prickly cactus in times of drought.

SAN JOAQUIN KIT FOX
Big ears help a kit fox pick up the tiniest sound when hunting prey.

DESERT KINGSNAKE
Kingsnakes kill lizards, other snakes, birds, and small mammals. They wrap their bodies around their victim and squeeze tightly until the animal can't breathe.

DESERT SCORPION
Scorpions catch, grip, and tear apart prey with their large front pincers.

DESERT TARANTULA
Tarantulas look scary, but their poison is no stronger than a bee's sting.

TURKEY VULTURE
A keen sense of smell helps the turkey vulture find the dead animals it eats. It will also kill small animals itself, and eat eggs and young birds.

ROADRUNNER
Roadrunners don't fly much. Instead, they run very fast, using their tail to steer around bushes, or as a brake when they screech to a halt.

CACTUS WREN
This wren's tough feathers and scaly legs protect it as it nests among cacti.

North American Everglades

APPLE SNAILS
In times of drought, this snail survives by digging deep into moist undersoil and sleeping.

ALLIGATOR
The alligator creates a ready food supply. It makes big holes in swamps called "gator holes," which fill with fish.

ZEBRA BUTTERFLY
A zebra butterfly's body contains poison from food it ate when still a caterpillar. This helps protect it from enemies.

PAINTED BUNTING
The male bunting uses its color to attract a mate, while the female is green to disguise her on the nest.

ORB WEAVER SPIDER
This spider injects its prey with a paralyzing venom. The prey then stays fresh until the spider eats it.

BROWN PELICAN
The brown pelican dives headfirst into the sea. It scoops up a huge mouthful of fish and water that can weigh up to twice as much as it does itself!

GREEN TREE FROG
Most tree frogs can change their color and pattern in response to light, moisture, and temperature.

RED-EARED TERRAPIN
These terrapins often climb out of the water to bask in huge piles several turtles deep.

North American Everglades

SNAPPING TURTLE
With its algae-covered shell, the snapping turtle is hard to spot as it lurks under the mud at the bottom of a pond. It waits to snatch unsuspecting frogs and fish with its ferocious bite.

ROSEATE SPOONBILL
The spoonbill sweeps its large bill through muddy water, snapping it shut when it scoops up a fish.

CORN SNAKE
Corn snakes are climbers. They lay up to 20 eggs at one time. The adults eat rodents and birds, but the young prefer a meal of frogs.

GREEN DARNER DRAGONFLY
Transparent wings and a twig-shaped body camouflage the darner.

EASTERN LUBBER GRASSHOPPER
This grasshopper spits out a stream of leaf pieces when threatened.

MANATEE
This rare creature lives entirely in the water. It uses its flat tail to push itself through water at speeds over 16 mi (26 km) per hour.

GARPIKE
Garpike breathe underwater using gills, but they can also breathe air if the swamp waters dry up.

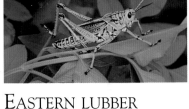

RED-SIDED GARTER SNAKE
This snake's skin expands like a balloon, allowing it to swallow large prey.

FIDDLER CRAB
This crab eats by putting balls of mud in its mouth, sieving out any edibles, and spitting out the rest.

Central American Rain Forests and Islands

GOLDEN BEETLE
A golden beetle's shiny wings glitter in the sunshine, making it difficult for enemies to spot it.

JUNGLE OCELOT
The rare jungle ocelot comes out at night to hunt birds, snakes, and small mammals.

CUBAN BEE HUMMINGBIRD
This is the tiniest bird in the world. It beats its wings so quickly they make a humming sound.

ST. VINCENT PARROT
These parrots fly around their forest home in flocks, looking for fruit, flowers, and seeds to eat.

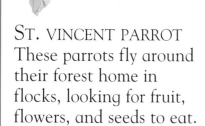

SALLYLIGHTFOOT CRAB
This crab's hard shell protects it from hungry birds. It scuttles sideways to avoid tripping over its many legs.

WOODPECKER FINCH
This clever bird pokes a twig under tree bark to dig out insect grubs to eat.

GALÁPAGOS PENGUIN
Galápagos penguins spend hours fishing, then flop onto sandy beaches to rest. They make their nests in caves or crevices.

FER-DE-LANCE SNAKE
The fer-de-lance is a very poisonous snake. It strikes victims quickly, injecting them with a paralyzing venom.

GLASS FROG
A glass frog has a see-through belly. It lays its eggs on leaves hanging over a stream. The tadpoles fall straight into the water when they hatch out.

Central American Rain Forests and Islands

GIANT TORTOISE
Giant tortoises live on the Galápagos Islands. They can go for a long time without food or water, and are good at moving over rough ground. They live for a long time, often up to 100 years.

KINKAJOU
A kinkajou swings from tree to tree, gripping at branches with its strong tail. Its favorite snack is honey from beehives – that's why it is also called a honey bear.

SOLENODON
This rare animal is found only on the island of Cuba. It kills lizards, rodents, and small birds for food and is one of the very few mammals that has a poisonous bite.

QUETZAL
This lovely bird lives right at the top of the trees in rain forests. The male's long, streamerlike tail feathers flutter and swirl as he shows off to attract a mate.

NINE-BANDED ARMADILLO
All of an armadillo's body, except for its belly, is covered in protective plates.

MAGNIFICENT FRIGATE BIRD
A male frigate bird inflates its throat pouch during its mating display to attract attention and impress female birds.

HOWLER MONKEY
The male howler monkey shouts at rival monkeys, warning them to stay away from its territory. Its roar can be heard up to 2 mi (3 km) away.

VAMPIRE BAT
A vampire bat slices the skin of its prey with its razor-sharp teeth, then laps up blood from the wound.

South American Pampas

CAVY
An ancestor of the pet guinea pig, the cavy prefers to use other animals' burrows or hide among rocks rather than dig its own shelter. It munches on berries and other plants.

CRESTED CARACARA
A caracara will peck and bully a vulture until it coughs up its food. This provides the caracara with a quick snack.

GIANT ANTEATER
A giant anteater rips open termite nests with its claws. Then it licks up the termites with its long, sticky tongue.

RED-CRESTED CARDINAL
A lively, bold bird with a melodious song, the cardinal is usually seen in small groups, pecking at seeds on the ground.

MANED WOLF
The maned wolf has long legs that are ideal for chasing prey through long grass. It deters predators by raising its mane to look bigger.

RHEA
Rheas are good swimmers and visit lakes and rivers to bathe in large groups.

PAMPAS DEER
Pampas deer have been widely hunted for their meat and horns and now very few are left. The male leaves a mating signal with a liquid that is so strong it can be smelled more than 1 mi (2 km) away.

MARAS
Maras live in groups in big underground burrows. When in danger, they will flash the white patch underneath their tails to warn each other of trouble.

South American Andes

TORRENT DUCK
The torrent duck's sharp claws help it grip slippery rocks while it feeds in fast-flowing, turbulent streams.

ANDEAN TAPIR
The tapir's trunk is more than just an extra-long nose. It uses it as a hand to tear off leaves to eat.

ANDEAN CONDOR
One of the largest flying birds, the condor cruises long distances looking for dead animals on which to feed.

SOUTHERN PUDU
About as tall as a spaniel dog, this shy little deer lives in remote areas and is seldom seen.

CHINCHILLA
A chinchilla's fur kept it warm in the cold mountains where it once lived. Now, most chinchillas are farmed for their fur.

GUANACO
Guanacos live in small herds with a single male adult. If danger threatens, the male bleats a warning and the rest of the group takes to its heels.

SPECTACLED BEAR
Each one of these bears has different spectacle-shaped markings around its eyes. The bears are good climbers and sleep in nests in trees.

VICUNA
Vicunas eat mainly grass, but they also lick stones and rocks for salt.

South American Rain Forests

THORN BUG
This bug keeps hungry birds away by looking just like a spiky thorn.

HORNED TOAD
When attacked, a horned toad squirts poison at its enemies from behind its eyes.

BLUE MORPHO BUTTERFLY
The tiny scales on the male butterfly's wings catch the sunlight, creating different colors as it flutters.

SPIDER MONKEY
A spider monkey uses its tail like an extra hand to grip branches as it leaps through trees.

JAGUAR
A jaguar's spotted coat blends in with its jungle surroundings, helping it sneak up on prey. It often hunts near water, attacking turtles and peccaries.

SLOTH
Slow-moving sloths hang upside down in the tops of trees, where they munch on leaves. They can hardly walk on the ground and may live in the same tree for years at a time.

PIRANHAS
When hundreds of sharp-toothed piranhas gather to attack, they can kill a large animal in minutes.

POISON DART FROG
This tiny frog's colorful skin warns enemies of the lethal poison it contains.

POSTMAN CATERPILLAR
This caterpillar feeds on passion fruit flowers. It stores poison from them in its body, so hungry predators aren't likely to eat it.

CAIMAN
Caimans lurk beneath the water, waiting to snatch passing animals.

South American Rain Forests

HERCULES BEETLE
The hercules beetle is thought to be the longest in the world – it can grow up to 7 in (18 cm).

GIANT ARMADILLO
A giant armadillo has the biggest front claws of any animal. It uses them to dig for worms, ants, and termites on the forest floor.

TOUCAN
The toucan uses its strong, hollow bill to reach fruit on twigs that are too small to hold the weight of its body.

GOLDEN LION TAMARIN
These tamarins have beautiful golden manes. They eat fruit and live in small groups. At night, they cuddle up together to sleep.

SCARLET MACAW
This large parrot splits open nutshells with its strong, razor-sharp beak. It uses its foot like a hand to hold food up to its mouth.

CAPYBARA
The largest of all rodents, the capybara always lives near water. When alarmed, it jumps into the water and swims beneath the surface to safety.

HARPY EAGLE
The harpy flies through the treetops at high speeds, chasing and snatching monkeys and other animals to eat.

EMERALD TREE BOA
This boa's bright green skin helps it hide among leaves and get close to its prey before it strikes. Then it uses its powerful muscles to suffocate its prey.

African Deserts

DORCAS GAZELLE
Dorcas gazelles usually graze early or late in the day, when it's cool.

SPINY-TAILED AGAMA
If an agama is attacked, it dives into its burrow, sticks its tail out of the top, and thrashes it from side to side to scare off the attacker.

DABB LIZARD
This lizard prefers plant food, but will eat insects when plants are scarce.

DROMEDARY
This type of camel can go without water for longer than any other animal. Its hump contains fat, which the camel uses as an energy store.

ADDAX
An addax almost never drinks. It gets all the moisture it needs from eating plants.

SPITTING COBRA
When this cobra gets scared, it rears up and spits venom.

FENNEC FOX
This tiny fox has huge ears. It can hear the slightest noise – even prey moving underground.

SOOTY FALCON
The sooty falcon preys on birds from Europe that fly south for winter. It pounces on them when they stop for a rest on their long journey.

African Deserts

Horned Viper
An angry horned viper will rub its scales together to make a loud, rasping noise. It paralyzes its prey with powerful venom.

Jerboa
Like a tiny kangaroo, the jerboa can leap huge distances on its powerful back legs. It uses its long tail to help it balance.

Locust
A locust is covered in a waterproof layer of wax, which prevents it from drying out in the burning desert sun.

Oryx
Large herds of up to 40 scimitar-horned oryx feed on grass at the edge of the desert.

Lanner Falcon
Lanner falcons use their sharp, curved talons to snatch small birds, bats, and flying insects in midair.

Sandgrouse
Sandgrouse chicks cannot fly to water holes, so they suck water from their father's belly feathers.

Caracal
This wild cat is a powerful jumper. It can even catch a low-flying bird by leaping high into the air.

Desert scorpion
A sting from this scorpion's tail releases poison as strong as a cobra's.

African Rain Forests and Lakes

AFRICAN JACANA
The jacana's long toes spread its weight so it can walk on floating water plants.

BLACK-AND-WHITE COLOBUS MONKEY
This tree-dwelling monkey moves with great ease and takes huge leaps between branches.

SILVERBACK GORILLA
Gorillas live in family groups on the ground, sometimes climbing trees to build nests. Adult males are called silverbacks because of the silvery hair that grows on their backs.

GIANT TIGER CENTIPEDE
A centipede scuttles through the jungle undergrowth, hunting insects and spiders to eat. It grabs its prey and injects poison with its large claws.

GIANT AFRICAN SNAIL
This snail is a giant, growing longer than 13 in (33 cm). It uses its tongue to scrape off bits of leaves to eat.

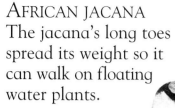

ROYAL ANTELOPE
The tiniest antelope in the world, the timid royal antelope is no bigger than a rabbit, with legs as thin as pencils.

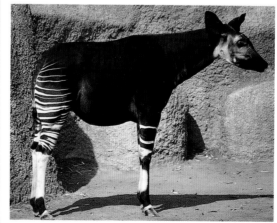

OKAPI
The shy okapi lives deep in the forest. Like its cousin, the giraffe, its tongue is so long it can use it to clean its eyes.

African Rain Forests and Lakes

GOLIATH FROG
This frog uses its powerful back legs to escape from attackers. It can cover 9 ft (3 m) in a single, enormous jump. That's the length of a car!

LEOPARD
Leopards rest in trees during the day and hunt at night. They drag their prey up into trees to keep other animals from eating it.

DE BRAZZA'S MONKEY
Long, strong arms and legs help this monkey run along the tops of tree branches and take huge, flying leaps from one tree to another.

AFRICAN CIVET
The civet eats just about anything it finds – insects, plants, and dead animals.

WATTLED BLACK HORNBILL
The female hornbill seals herself and her chicks in her nest with mud. The male pokes food through a slit until the chicks are ready to fly.

HIPPOPOTAMUS
A hippopotamus spends much of the day in water, walking rather than swimming along the riverbed.

CHIMPANZEE
Chimpanzees eat mainly fruit, but they will also use twigs to poke termites out of their nests.

African Savanna

GIRAFFE
A giraffe reaches high into trees to tear leaves from the branches with its long tongue.

AARDVARK
An aardvark spends its days asleep in its deep burrow. It comes out at night to feast on termites.

BLACK RHINOCEROS
Despite its bulky body, the black rhinoceros is fairly agile. It can gallop at up to 30 mi (48 kph) over short distances.

HONEY BADGER
This badger gets its name from its favorite food – honey!

RUPPELL'S GRIFFON VULTURES
Sharp-eyed vultures gather in big flocks to feed on carcasses.

OLIVE BABOON
A baboon walks along on all fours, looking for fruit, roots, bulbs, or eggs to crunch up with its strong, sharp teeth.

SERVAL
The long-legged serval moves easily through tall grass as it hunts rodents and birds.

OSTRICH
The ostrich is the biggest bird in the world. It cannot fly, but it can run faster than a racehorse.

RED-HEADED WEAVER
The male bird weaves a thick-walled nest of grasses for its chicks.

African Savanna

LION
A lion's family group is called a pride. The females hunt, while the males protect the pride.

RUNNING FROGS
These frogs walk rather than hop. They feed on insects and make a noise like a popping cork.

MARABOU STORK
A marabou's bald head is easy to keep clean, which is useful because this bird feeds on messy carcasses.

GEMSBOKS
Straight-horned gemsboks graze on grassy plains in large groups.

HYENA
A hyena's jaws are strong enough to crunch up an animal carcass, bones and all. Hyenas usually feed on animals killed by others, but will also hunt in packs at night.

AFRICAN ELEPHANT
The largest land animal, an African elephant has to eat plants for up to 16 hours a day just to get enough nutrients.

IMPALAS
Impalas live in herds of females, their young, and one adult male. Other males form smaller herds.

NILE CROCODILE
Like a floating log, the crocodile lurks in shallow water, waiting for an animal to come for a drink. Then it surges out and clamps its victim in its powerful jaws.

African Savanna

PORCUPINE
When a porcupine is attacked, it raises its sharp, hollow quills and rattles them fiercely. It then turns its back, and sticks its quills into the enemy's skin.

CROWNED CRANE
Cranes wade through long grass, searching for an insect meal.

SENEGAL BUSHBABY
Bushbabies use their nimble hands to catch flying insects, build nests, and defend themselves.

ZEBRA
Zebras use their hooves to fend off attackers. A stallion's kick is so powerful it can smash a lion's teeth.

CAPE BUFFALO
Buffalo must drink every day, so buffalo herds are never far from water holes.

THOMSON'S GAZELLE
If a gazelle herd gets scared, the gazelles all stiffen their legs and jump up and down. This is called "pronking," and may confuse an attacker.

CHEETAH
The cheetah is the fastest land animal, but it tires easily, so it uses short bursts of speed when chasing prey.

VERVET MONKEYS
Vervets live in big groups, often of more than 100. They call out to warn one another of danger.

Madagascan Rain Forests

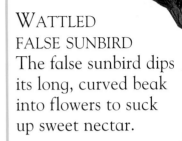

MOON MOTH
The moon moth comes out at night. The spots on its wings look like an animal's eyes and help fool predators.

STRIPED CIVET
The civet is active only at night. It feeds mainly on aquatic animals but also eats rodents.

WATTLED FALSE SUNBIRD
The false sunbird dips its long, curved beak into flowers to suck up sweet nectar.

AYE-AYE
An aye-aye uses its long, bony middle finger to pull grubs from under bark or pulp from coconuts.

INDRI
Indris are very big lemurs. They make loud wails that can be heard up to 2 mi (3 km) away.

PARSON'S CHAMELEON
The chameleon changes color when a rival enters its territory or when it is trying to attract a mate. It has pincerlike hands and feet that help it grip branches.

MADAGASCAN DAY GECKO
As this gecko grows, its skin gets too tight. So it grows another skin underneath, scrapes off the old skin, and eats it.

RING-TAILED LEMUR
Big groups of these lemurs snuggle together when it is cool.

TOMATO FROGS
Tomato frogs are so-called because of their plump, round shape and bright orange-red skin color.

EUROPEAN ROLLER

The roller's name comes from its courtship antics in the air. It rolls from side to side as it swoops and dives.

CHAMOIS

Chamois live on high mountains. Soft pads on each hoof help them grip the rocks.

HOOPOE

A young hoopoe deters an attacker by producing a foul-smelling liquid.

SMALL-SPOTTED GENET

A genet's excellent eyesight, sense of smell, and hearing make it a good hunter. It comes out at night to catch small mammals.

EGYPTIAN VULTURE

Egyptian vultures breed in Europe in the summer. They fly to Africa in the winter.

PRAYING MANTIS

A mantis produces a foam in which it lays its eggs. The foam then hardens to protect the eggs.

BROWN BEAR

In fall, bears eat lots of berries and nuts to get fat for winter. They spend winter asleep in caves.

IBERIAN WOLF

These animals shelter in dens made in holes in the ground or in caves.

MONK SEAL

This seal is now very rare because its seaside homes have been taken over by vacationers.

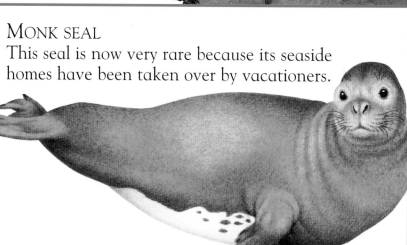

Southern European Mountains and Scrub

GOLDEN ORIOLE
The male oriole's bright colors help it attract a female. The female makes an intricate nest, like a hammock slung between two twigs.

BARBARY APE
These tailless apes live only on the Rock of Gibraltar. They may have been brought there by the Romans.

PEREGRINE FALCON
This falcon hunts other birds, striking them in midair with its feet.

COMMON SHREW
The common shrew has to eat almost nonstop or it will starve.

GREEN TOAD
The green toad lives in dry, sandy places. It has no teeth, so it swallows its food whole.

EUROPEAN BROWN HARE
A hare usually walks along, eating plants. But if it is chased, it runs at top speed, with just the tips of its feet touching the ground.

KESTREL
A kestrel hovers high in the air, scanning the ground for rodents to snatch with its sharp claws.

SPANISH LYNX
Lynx live alone and hunt at night. There are very few left in Europe. Many have been killed for their fur, and most of their forest homes have been destroyed.

FLAMINGO
Flamingos stir up the muddy bottoms of lakes with their webbed feet to find shrimps to eat.

European Deciduous Forests

EUROPEAN BADGER
Badgers are shy animals. They live in burrows, or setts, which they dig with the long claws on their strong front legs. They can close their ears and nostrils to keep out dirt while digging.

WEASEL
A weasel can squeeze into burrows to catch moles and mice. It also climbs trees to eat birds' eggs and nestlings.

HOVERFLY
Many hoverflies look like bees or wasps. This disguise stops birds from eating them.

MOLE
Moles are skilled tunnelers – they are nearly blind, but have big, scooplike forefeet.

NUTHATCH
A nuthatch wedges a nut in tree bark, then hammers it with its beak to crack the shell. It also climbs headfirst down trees, hunting for insects under the bark.

TAWNY OWL
This owl's soft-fringed wing feathers help it fly silently at night when hunting.

EUROPEAN FIRE SALAMANDER
Salamanders take in oxygen through their damp skin. They are happier on land than in water, and like to shelter under logs in the woods.

GRAY SQUIRREL
Gray squirrels live in British woods, hoarding nuts for the winter.

HEDGEHOG
A hedgehog uses its sharp spines to protect its soft underparts from predators.

European Deciduous Forests

LADYBUG
These beetles love to munch plant pests called aphids. Their bright red color warns enemies that they taste bitter.

RED FOX
Originally woodland animals, now many foxes live in towns, raiding dumpsters in search of food scraps.

STRIPED-WINGED GRASSHOPPER
This grasshopper makes a high-pitched whine by rubbing its back legs against its front wings.

BLUE TIT
Busy blue tit parents bring their chicks more than 10,000 items of food while they are in the nest.

YELLOW-NECKED WOODMOUSE
The woodmouse is the largest mouse. The female has up to 32 babies in a year.

BUMBLEBEE
A bumblebee sometimes collects so much pollen in the sacs on its back legs that it struggles to fly.

DORMOUSE
In fall, a dormouse eats enough to double its weight, which helps it survive its long winter sleep.

GREATER SPOTTED WOODPECKER
This bird pecks deep into tree bark with its beak and then reaches into cracks to lick up insects with its tongue.

FALLOW DEER
The fallow deer's spotted summer coat helps it hide in the dappled light of the forest. The males have antlers, which they use for fighting.

WILD BOAR
The wild boar uses its long, sensitive nose to snuffle for roots, mushrooms, and bulbs on the forest floor.

European Coniferous Forests

WILDCAT
The European wildcat looks much like a big domestic cat, but it has heavier, shorter legs and a thick, stripy tail. It comes out at night to hunt for prey such as rabbits, birds, and insects.

CAPERCAILLIE
A male capercaillie shows off to females by sticking out its neck, fanning its tail, and making a gurgling noise.

EUROPEAN WOLF
Wolves hunt in packs, using their good sense of smell to sniff out prey.

OSPREY
The osprey dives feetfirst into water to grab fish with its strong claws. It can carry a fish weighing up to 4 lb (2 kg).

RED DEER
During the breeding season, or rut, a male red deer uses its antlers to fight other male rivals.

ICHNEUMON FLY
An ichneumon fly is a parasite that lays eggs in or on other animals.

PINE MARTEN
A pine marten takes such big jumps through the trees that it looks like it's flying. Its bushy tail helps it balance.

RED SQUIRREL
An agile acrobat, this little squirrel's hooked claws and strong legs help it scamper down trees headfirst.

Asian Tropical Forests

INDIAN DESERT CAT
This desert cat hunts small animals such as mice and lizards.

BORNEO FRUIT BAT
A fruit bat's keen sense of smell helps it find fruit to eat.

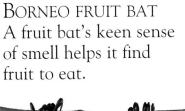

BENGAL EAGLE OWL
Active night and day, this owl uses its sharp eyesight to hunt a range of prey, from small insects to large birds. It has a deep, hooting call.

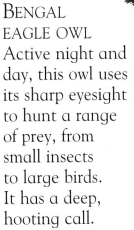

WILD WATER BUFFALO
Buffalo spend their time wading in marshes or swamps and eating grass.

BABIRUSA
A babirusa has four tusks, two of which grow right through its top lip.

PURPLE GALLINULE
The gallinule spreads out its long toes to stop it from sinking into mud while looking for food. It seldom flies, preferring to hide or dive to escape enemies.

PEACOCK
The fan of gorgeous feathers above the male peacock's tail is used to attract females, but molts after the breeding season.

ATLAS MOTH
The eyelike spots on this moth's wings distract enemies, who aim at the "eyes" and miss the body.

ASIAN ELEPHANT
Elephants live in herds led by an older female. They use their long trunks like hands to pick up food to eat, and as hoses to spray themselves with water.

Asian Tropical Forests

KING COBRA
Although usually mild-mannered, the venom of an angry cobra can kill a human in 15 to 20 minutes.

RHESUS MACAQUE MONKEYS
Rhesus macaques live in groups of up to 35, led by a female.

MALAYAN TAPIR
This tapir escapes from its enemies by hiding underwater and using its trunk just like a snorkel, poking it out to breathe.

STARRED TORTOISE
A starred tortoise uses its high, knobbly shell for defense against its predators. It draws its head and legs into the shell for protection.

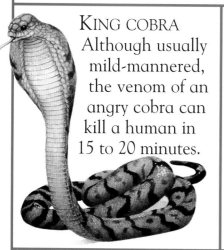

ALEXANDRINE PARAKEET
With its powerful beak, this parakeet can cause a lot of damage to crops, flowers, and fruit.

MALAYAN SUN BEAR
The smallest bear, the sun bear is active only at night. It spends its days snoozing in nests in trees and basking in the sun.

PROBOSCIS MONKEY
The male proboscis's big nose swells up and turns red when it gets angry.

KOMODO DRAGON
The largest lizard in the world, the Komodo eats goats, monkeys, deer, and even people.

TOKAY GECKO
Sticky pads on this gecko's toes help it climb up vertical surfaces. It gets its name from the loud "to-kay" noise it makes.

Asian Tropical Forests

HANGING PARROT
These parrots get their name from their habit of hanging upside down from a branch to rest.

MUDSKIPPER
This strange fish spends lots of time out of water. It breathes by filling its gill pouches with water and using the oxygen in it.

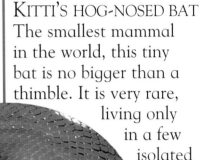

INDIAN RHINOCEROS
Thick folds of skin cover this rhino like a suit of armor. They protect it from thorns, ticks, and even tigers.

MANGROVE RAT SNAKE
This snake waits at the mouth of a cave with its mouth wide open. It grabs bats that fly past its head, then slowly suffocates them.

KITTI'S HOG-NOSED BAT
The smallest mammal in the world, this tiny bat is no bigger than a thimble. It is very rare, living only in a few isolated caves.

TIGER
The biggest wild cat of all, the tiger is an awesome and powerful beast. It hunts alone, attacking large prey such as cattle.

LION-TAILED MACAQUE
This macaque is a good climber. It is as happy in water as it is on land.

GLIDING GECKO
This gecko glides by catching the air with spread-out flaps of skin on its sides.

ORANGUTAN
An orangutan's long arms reach its ankles. It uses them for swinging through the trees. It builds itself a new tree nest to sleep in each night.

Asian Forests, Mountains, and Steppes

RED PANDA
A red panda comes out at night to eat plants. It washes by licking one of its paws and wiping it over its face.

BLUE MAGPIE
Magpies hop across clearings to hunt snails, lizards, centipedes, and even small snakes.

PRZEWALSKI'S HORSE
Only a few of these wild horses still live in their natural habitat on the steppes of central Asia.

GIANT PANDA
Pandas are great bamboo eaters. Their throats have an extra-thick lining to protect them from sharp splinters when swallowing bamboo stalks.

TAKIN
A takin looks like an ox, goat, sheep, and antelope rolled into one. Its strong legs help it climb the steep, rocky slopes of the Himalayan mountains, where it lives in big herds.

LADY AMHERST'S PHEASANT
A shy bird that seldom leaves its mountain home, this pheasant eats mostly bamboo shoots, with only the occasional spider or earwig meal.

JAPANESE MACAQUE
Troops of Japanese macaques keep warm in winter by sitting in hot volcanic springs with water right up to their necks.

URAL OWL
This owl's call can be heard up to 1 mi (2 km) away.

MONGOLIAN GERBIL
These gerbils don't need to drink. They get all the liquid they need from the seeds that they cram into their cheek pouches.

Asian Forests, Mountains, and Steppes

BAIKAL SEALS
These seals live in Lake Baikal, Siberia. They are the only seals to live in freshwater rather than seawater.

BOBAK MARMOT
Marmots live in big groups. One of them always stands guard to warn the others of danger.

ASIATIC BLACK BEAR
In fall, black bears eat a lot so that they grow really fat. They use this fat store to survive the winter, when food is scarce.

MUSK DEER
The male musk deer produces a liquid that is used to make perfume.

MANDARIN DUCK
During the day, this shy woodland duck rests in trees that overhang water. It feeds at dusk.

DWARF HAMSTER
These relatives of pet hamsters still live wild in burrows on the steppe.

BACTRIAN CAMEL
A bactrian camel grows a thick, shaggy coat to keep warm in the icy Gobi Desert winter. In summer, when the desert is scorching hot, it sheds most of its hair.

YAK
High up in the Himalayas, there are still a few wild yaks. Despite their massive size, they are nimble and surefooted, living happily on steep slopes.

SNOW LEOPARD
A powerful wild cat, the snow leopard can leap across ravines. It lives alone in the mountains, hunting wild sheep and goats at night.

Australalasian Rain Forests and Deciduous Forests

GRAY KANGAROO
Kangaroos live in groups called mobs. Their babies are called joeys.

SUGAR GLIDER
Sugar gliders love to eat the sugary sap of eucalyptus trees.

TREE KANGAROO
This kangaroo uses its sharp claws to climb trees. It returns to the ground by sliding down tail-first.

PLATYPUS
The platypus has a ducklike bill that it uses to probe for small aquatic animals to eat.

SULFUR-CRESTED COCKATOO
This cockatoo often looks grubby because it scratches in the dusty earth for seeds, roots, bulbs, and fruit to eat.

MOUNTAIN BRUSHTAIL OPOSSSUM
This opossum is usually found snoozing in a hollow of an eucalyptus tree.

KOOKABURRA
A kookaburra's laughing call isn't friendly – it tells other birds to stay away.

KING BIRD OF PARADISE
The male king bird is shy, but he puffs himself up and screams when trying to attract a mate.

TIGER CAT
This animal is not a cat at all. It is a marsupial – an animal whose babies are carried in the mother's pouch after they are born.

Australasian Rain Forests and Deciduous Forests

WHITE'S TREE FROG
Sticky disks on this frog's toes help it cling to tree branches. Its loose, floppy skin folds over branches and also helps it grip.

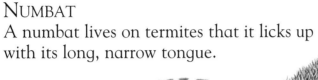

TASMANIAN DEVIL
This marsupial has powerful jaws and can crunch up a carcass, bones and all.

EASTERN ROSELLA
The beautiful rosella flies close to the ground in pairs or small groups.

NUMBAT
A numbat lives on termites that it licks up with its long, narrow tongue.

FUNNEL-WEB SPIDER
This deadly spider lurks in its burrow, waiting to poison its prey.

RINGTAIL OPOSSUM
This opossum gets its name from the way it curls its tail up. It also uses its tail as an extra hand when climbing trees.

KOALA
Koalas eat only certain eucalyptus leaves. A baby koala lives in its mother's pouch for up to eight months. After that it is carried on her back.

RAGGIANA'S BIRD OF PARADISE
The male bird uses his amazing plumage to attract a female. He even hangs upside down in trees to better show off his feathers.

Australian Outback

MULGARA
Even though it is small in size, the fierce mulgara attacks almost any small animal it finds – mouse, bird, or lizard.

ECHIDNA
When an echidna is attacked, it rolls into a ball with its sharp spines stuck out and its head and tummy tucked out of sight. It has a sticky tongue that it uses to snatch prey.

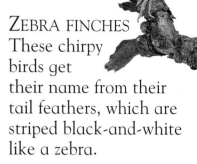

ZEBRA FINCHES
These chirpy birds get their name from their tail feathers, which are striped black-and-white like a zebra.

WESTERN QUOLL
The western quoll feeds on small animals and large insects, which it hunts both on the ground and in trees.

THORNY DEVIL
This prickly lizard eats ants, scooping up hundreds with one lick of its sticky tongue.

RED KANGAROO
With its enormous and powerful back legs, this kangaroo is able to take massive single leaps of more than 30 ft (9 m) – longer than three cars parked end to end. It uses its big, heavy tail to help it balance as it bounds along.

DINGO
The dingo hunts for carrion and small prey alone, but joins with other dingoes to hunt wallabies.

GALAH
The most common parrots in Australia, huge flocks of screeching galahs gather to roost in trees.

BLUE-TONGUED LIZARD
This lizard discourages attackers by sticking out its bright blue tongue and hissing loudly.

Australian Outback

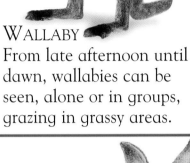

EASTERN QUOLL
This quoll is nocturnal. It sleeps all day in hollow logs.

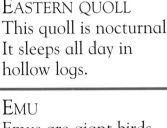

MARSUPIAL MOLE
A marsupial mole is so well-adapted to life in dark underground tunnels that it has lost its sight.

WALLABY
From late afternoon until dawn, wallabies can be seen, alone or in groups, grazing in grassy areas.

EMU
Emus are giant birds. They can't fly, but they are good swimmers and runners. The female lays eggs, which the male keeps warm until they hatch. He also keeps an eye on the chicks until they are more than a year old.

MALLEE FOWL
The female mallee lays eggs in a pile of rotting plants, which keeps them warm until they hatch.

FAT-TAILED DUNNART
The dunnart eats the equivalent of its own body weight in insects every day. It stores fat in its tail for energy.

RABBIT-EARED BANDICOOT
This marsupial does a lot of burrowing, digging burrows up to 7 ft (2 m) deep with its strong claws.

GOULD'S MONITOR LIZARD
More than 3 ft (1 m) long, this lizard eats all sorts of animal foods, but its favorite meal is eggs.

HAIRY-NOSED WOMBAT
The hairy-nosed wombat keeps cool during the hot desert days by staying in its burrow. It eats mainly grass, and can go without a drink for months at a time.

Coral Reef

ELECTRIC RAY
A ray hugs prey with its pectoral fins, then kills its victim with a massive electric shock from muscles on either side of its head.

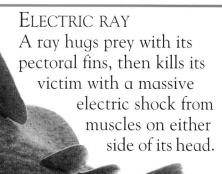

CROWN-OF-THORNS STARFISH
The crown-of-thorns starfish feeds on corals. It is well protected by its fearsome spines.

GIANT BLUE CLAM
Giant clams can live for hundreds of years. They open their shell to feed, but slam it shut when in danger.

COMMON STARFISH
A starfish sticks its stomach out of its mouth and pours digestive juices onto prey. It then enfolds it in its stomach and eats it.

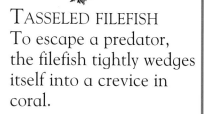

TASSELED FILEFISH
To escape a predator, the filefish tightly wedges itself into a crevice in coral.

PORCUPINEFISH
A porcupinefish can blow up its body to two or three times its normal size to scare away enemies.

BLACKTIP REEF SHARK
The reef shark has rows of scissor-sharp teeth to tear chunks of flesh off its victims' bones.

COPPERBANDED BUTTERFLYFISH
The copper-banded butterflyfish uses its long snout to pick out food from corals.

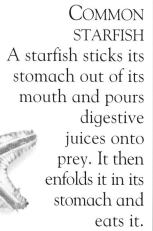

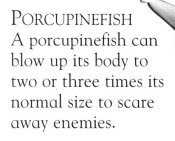

YELLOW TANG
Incredibly tiny yellow scales on this tang's body give it a soft, velvety appearance.

SEA CUCUMBER
A sea cucumber's sticky tentacles catch tiny animals and plants as it crawls over coral.

Coral Reef

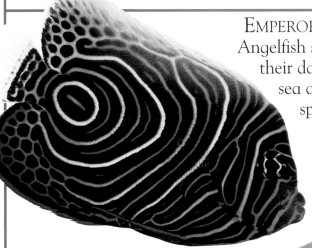

EMPEROR ANGELFISH
Angelfish spend most of their day nibbling on sea animals called sponges. When two angelfish mate, they stay together for the rest of their lives.

SMOOTH BRAIN CORAL
Corals cannot move, so they rely on the movement of seawater to bring food to them.

SEA FAN
This plantlike sea animal sticks to rocks using a special organ called a holdfast.

TEARDROP BUTTERFLYFISH
Each type of butterflyfish has a different diet and home, so they don't compete for food.

SEA SLUG
Sea slugs have no shells to protect their soft bodies. Instead, they taste horrible, which deters hungry hunters.

LIONFISH
The deadly lionfish has spiny fins with glands that make a powerful poison to deter predators.

SEA SQUIRTS
While still young, a squirt swims around, but as an adult, it attaches itself to a rock where it sucks in microorganisms to eat.

BLUE DEVIL FISH
Each scale of this brilliant blue fish has a tiny yellow-white mark in the middle.

CLOWNFISH
A clownfish is not harmed by a sea anemone's poisonous sting, so it can seek safety from predators among an anemone's tentacles.

HERMIT CRAB
A hermit crab lives in another creature's empty shell to stay safe from predators. When it grows too big for its shell, it moves into a bigger one.

The Antarctic

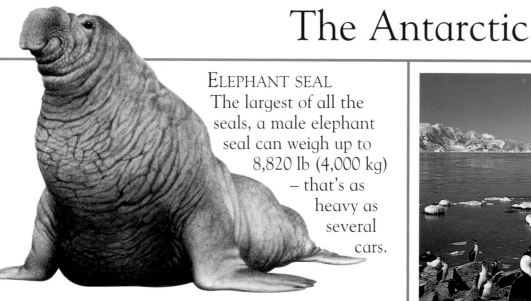

ELEPHANT SEAL
The largest of all the seals, a male elephant seal can weigh up to 8,820 lb (4,000 kg) – that's as heavy as several cars.

KING PENGUINS
Both male and female king penguins warm the female's egg on their feet.

MACARONI PENGUINS
Macaroni penguins move on land by hopping. This is the perfect way for them to climb steep slopes to reach their nests, built in cliffs above the ocean.

BLUE-EYED SHAGS
When this bird spots a fish in the ocean, it dives down at top speed and chases it along by swimming underwater.

GREAT SKUA
With their large, hooked bills, skuas are fierce predators. They attack and eat other seabirds.

WANDERING ALBATROSS
This albatross has the largest wingspan of any bird. It glides over the sea, looking for fish to eat.

KILLER WHALE
Killer whales, or orcas, live in groups called pods. They hunt and eat any animal they find – penguins, seals, fish, and even dolphins.

GENTOO PENGUINS
Gentoo penguins lay two eggs each year. Both the male and female keep the eggs warm until they hatch.

ANTARCTIC FUR SEAL
Bull fur seals are kind of like lions. They have a ruff of hair around their necks and roar loudly during the breeding season.

The Ocean

COWFISH
When viewed from the front, this fish looks like a cow. Its angular body is made up of bony plates rather than scales.

HAMMERHEAD SHARK
This shark has a T-shaped head with eyes on either side, giving it a wide range of vision. Its head shape also helps it steer through the water.

LOGGERHEAD TURTLE
The loggerhead turtle has jaws that are powerful enough to crush clams.

BLUE WHALE
The blue whale is the largest animal on Earth – it can grow as long as ten cars end to end. It breathes through a small hole on its head.

HI-HAT DRUMFISH
The drumming and knocking sounds of these fish carry far underwater.

BOTTLENOSE DOLPHIN
Living in large groups, or schools, these animals use high-pitched noises to talk to each other.

OCTOPUS
When chased, an octopus squirts out clouds of dark, inky liquid to escape from its attacker.

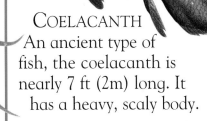

COELACANTH
An ancient type of fish, the coelacanth is nearly 7 ft (2m) long. It has a heavy, scaly body.

WOBBEGONG SHARK
This shark's flat shape and tasseled mouth have earned it the nickname "carpet shark."

Domestic Animals

DUCKLING
A duckling's down is made waterproof by the oil in its mother's feathers.

PARAKEET
Parakeets can be trained to do tricks. They can sometimes learn to mimic sounds.

DONKEY
Donkeys are often kept on farms to provide company for ponies.

SHETLAND PONY
Shetlands make perfect ponies for children because they are small and gentle natured.

SHIRE HORSE
These huge horses were once used to pull plows and heavy loads on farms.

CANARY
The canary is a very popular pet because of its beautiful song and bright coloring.

COW
Dairy cows produce an average of 3-4 gal (10-15 li) of milk each day.

LAMBS
Lambs are born in spring. A strong and healthy new-born lamb is on its feet just minutes after birth.

GOAT
Goats will climb almost anything to get food and they will eat almost anything – from grass to shoes! They are kept on farms for their milk.

Domestic Animals

LOP-EARED RABBIT
Like many other breeds, this rabbit is bred to be a domestic pet.

GUINEA PIG
There are many guinea pig breeds, with varied colors and hair types.

GOOSE
Geese make good guards, honking and cackling when strangers are around.

PIGS
A female pig, or sow, is able to feed up to 20 piglets at one time from her two lines of teats.

TURKEY
A male turkey attracts a female by making a gobbling noise, raising its tail feathers, and shaking its wing feathers.

HUSKY
An energetic dog, the husky is traditionally used to pull sleds in the Arctic.

BURMESE CAT
This short-haired Burmese is affectionate and enjoys human company.

MOUSE
Pet mice can be brown, like wild mice, or black, white, or patchy.

CHICKEN
This familiar farmyard bird can lay one or more eggs every day.

HAMSTER
Hamsters store food in special cheek pouches. They can eat it later.

DOG
A dog's sense of smell is so good that it can tell the emotional state of another animal from its odor.

47

Index

Ants are everywhere! A single queen ant can lay over 100,000 eggs in just a few days.